TROUBLE
behind glass doors

Also by Walter Bargen

TROUBLE
behind glass doors

poems

Walter Bargen

BkMk Press
University of Missouri-Kansas City

BkMk Press
University of Missouri-Kansas City
5101 Rockhill Road
Kansas City, Missouri 64110
(816) 235-2558 (voice) / (816) 235-2611 (fax)
www.umkc.edu/bkmk

Financial assistance for this project has been provided by the
Missouri Arts Council, a state agency.

Cover art: Mike Sleadd
Author photo: Taylor Galscock
Book interior design: Susan L. Schurman
Editorial Consultant: Karen I. Johnson
Managing editor: Ben Furnish

BkMk Press wishes to thank Linda D. Brennaman, Kevin Berndt,
Bradley Hoffman, Marie Mayhugh, Grace Stansbery.

Printing by Sheridan Books

Library of Congress Cataloging-in-Publication Data

Bargen, Walter.
  [Poems. Selections]
  Trouble Behind Glass Doors : Poems / Walter Bargen.—First Edition.
    pages cm
  ISBN 978-1-886157-87-3 (paperback : alk. paper)
  I. Title.
  PS3552.A6162T76 2013
  811'.54—dc23
                        2013020238

This book is set in Georgia and Handwriting-Dakota

The poems listed first appeared in the following journals and anthologies:

Black Rock & Sage Review	What Happens to Such People
Chance of a Ghost Anthology	Ghost Technology
Elder Mountain	North Ninth Street
Gingko Tree Review	Point of No Return
Ginosko	Apocalyptic Godiva
Hurricane Blues Anthology	Rescuers
I-70 Review	In Her Own Flight
	Games
Iron Horse Literary Review	Overdose
Little Balkans Review	Scantily Clad Poet
Melic Review	In These Times
Montserrat	Dyslexic Forest
New Letters	Derailed
	Poet in Prison
Permafrost	Errancy
Pleiades	The Whole Facts
Posse Review	Dying of Strangers
	(as "Refaceable")
Redaction	El Playon, San Salvador
River Styx	Poet as Grand Marshall of the Fall Parade
	Neighbors
Rockhurst Review	Where Hieronymus Washes His
	Hands
Stirring	Domino Coffee Shop
Valparaiso Review	Paperwork
	War Feathers
Whirly Bird Anthology	Meeting Frida Near the State
Of Kansas City Writers	Capitol

The poem "Hall of Waters" first appeared in the books *The Vertical River* and *The Body of Water* published by Timberline Press. It is the lyric for the choral composition by Amy Beth Kirsten for *Verses & Voices*.

The poem "Moon Walk" was written for the occasion of the appointment of the First Poet Laureate of Missouri, February 13, 2008.

"Poet as Grand Marshall of the Fall Parade" first appeared in the book *Endearing Ruins/Liebenswerte Ruinen* published by Liliom-Verlag, Germany, in a bilingual edition (translated by Josef Wittmann).

"University of Fields" was written for the occasion of the 100th anniversary of the University of Missouri's membership in the Association of American Universities.

TROUBLE
behind glass doors

3

Tribulations worketh patience; and patience experience; and experience hope.

—Paul, Romans 5: 3-4

. . . with their feet deep in the dust of the earth as desolate as the sky, they went along with the resigned look of men who are condemned to hope forever.

—Charles Baudelaire

Hope is infinite—but not for us.

—Franz Kafka

Dyslexic Forest

We plod along, grow slow,
slower than grass, and no higher
than September's dry reedy weeds
sighing on breezes.

We watch cows return at evening,
their measured gait a dirge,
a monkish line, their tails down,
heads bowed toward the barn.

The boy across the hollow
finds no porch at which to sit
and watch the aging lacquered light
of dusk, and to doze, if only for a moment,

then to startle awake, hearing the valley
clear its throat of fog.
He tells the school counselor
his doubts, his worries,

when asked why he falls asleep in class
each day. He says there's a writer
who lives across the hollow,
who walks the woods at night,

troubling the trees, standing so still a bobcat
sharpens its claws on his legs and he doesn't
flinch, who reads to the stones
and they listen hard all down the creek,

who calls to the clairvoyant moon
as clouds wail back warnings. He hears
the writer's voice: leafy humus, moist
and spongy, tangled with roots, beetle

and grub laden, fungus and worm swollen.
He hears it all each night, the rustle
of each step coming closer,

silhouettes of branches pointed as pens,

and he can't sleep in this growing commotion
of words.   Class is quieter, a plodding place.

Moon Walk

Not to forget what's important
I let the screen door slam behind me,
An alarm, an exclamation, an emphatic here,
Now. I inhale deeply, hear the flutter of wings.
My feet never leave the ground.
An awkward jump off the porch isn't flight.
Years of sky compress under foot.

Not even a first moon step,
Nothing for mankind, at best
A kind man. The moon double-barreling
Down light. The intensity of cosmic reflection
Like these worked words made to feel light,
Drawing out the indelible oak and hickory shadows,
A stark ink writing toward another season.

Winter's introduction long past,
Tonight's still cold.
A barred owl opens the booming forest
Of its voice. I enter but come
No closer to seeing it.
I have no bold moves left.
My small steps leave
Leaves little disturbed
in their decomposing dreams.

Four walls not enough.
Ceiling just another floor.
How can we live without
The belted sparkle of Orion
As he stalks forever?

The sky star pierced.
Constellations tattooed to their stories.
Such epics the accumulated wisdom
To our ends. The telling lives in us.
We are pierced that deeply.

Poet as Grand Marshal of the Fall Parade

Doubting the gravitas, the decorum, it's poetry after all,
and being led by a Boy Scout honor guard that's following a police car's
flashing lights, their brown shirts sashed with merit badges,
and behind them the poet bucket-seated in a low-riding wine-dark
      sports car.

From a small bag, he tosses candy to children who are wondering
why they're not watching Saturday morning cartoons, knowing
      Halloween
is a month off. Standing with their plastic Wal-Mart and Moser bags,
costumed in sleep they wake to the brash high school marching band
as it gracelessly plays what is half-remembered after so few weeks
of practice. The cough and clatter of two diesel tractors,
a wagon pulled by mules, another by horses, the women's garden club
armed with rakes and shovels, the women's Red Hat Society, a rabble
from the Chamber of Commerce, the mayor biking in circles
around the too slow procession, and whoever else joins in.

The poet agreed thinking this is what football players are adored into
      doing,
but he's never led a team to victory much less played, and he considered
      wearing
shoulder pads outside his suit with poems scrawled in inch-high letters
      on
the plastic, but he was afraid to confuse the mile-long, one-person-deep
      crowd
more than they already were as he passed out poems once the candy ran
      out.

University of Fields

Don't wait in the long hallway of the waiting world,
step into the open field across the pasture fence.
Let's meet where distant cattle punctuate the horizon

under the long sentence of blackbirds inscribing the too-blue sky.
At your feet the earth unfolds in white bouquets of daisy fleabane,
in asters streaming neon along the hoof-rutted paths.

Bruised with broomsedge the slope slips and settles by the shore.
The pond blinks under a solitary cloud pedestaled on its shadow.
From the long lashes of cattails a ghostly suited heron addresses
the air.

Along the tree line, fallen hedge apples think slowly into earth.
Profligate persimmons decorate branches. Seed into seed time
coldly collapses and flocks of cedar waxwings harvest berries.

Barred owl and red fox prepare. There is no waiting.
The hallways are crowded, the amalgam of lives clear
and strong and thriving within a country of associations.

Scantily Clad Poet

An editor of an online magazine tells the poet
that she examined their Google Analytics.
A new geometry of attention, the poet thinks,
that eluded Euclid: the axiom of how many people
visited the Web site, the hypotenuse of where
these visitors live, the theorem of what stories
are read, down to sequencing readers' keystrokes.

She has discovered that the poet is the second most popular
keyword used to search the Web site after the football team
and before the "Golden Girls" (not the TV sitcom).
In other words, she says, the poet is less popular than football
but more popular than scantily clad dancing college girls
cheering the team to victory. Who says poetry is dead?

Later she clarifies her earlier analysis in order to curb
the poet's enthusiasm. The poet is not the second
most-read story, that position belongs to a student named
by Glamour Magazine as one of the top-ten college
women of the year, but the poet is the more searched for.

Epistemologically, ontologically, profound implications,
but for others a poster on the post office bulletin board will do.
Then she suggests the rankings might have been different,
If the poet had been shot jumping up and down in a cute red dress.
Now the poet is hurt, red is not his favorite color.
Then the poet wonders what she meant by shot.

Poet in Prison

Home is where the heart gives out and we arouse the grass.

—James Galvin

I

Morning's cold blanket pulled back
in dull light. Blowing sheets of bitter wind.
Forecast snow.
Hawks perch on stunted snags beside ditches.
The shattered stubble of harvested fields
hobbles toward the horizon.
A metal building, Jane's Custom Designed Bras,
sits alone miles from any house or hand.
An ethanol plant's acronym is POET.
Recite biofuels. From the highway,
the flat-red buildings echo Kentucky horse barns
but are surrounded by twelve-feet-high fence
that curves inward, a glittering wave of chain-link
always in the act of crashing, topped with a froth
of churning razor wire. A landlocked ocean.

2

Space between airlock doors.
Space between the whoosh of opening and closing.
Space between windows stacked with concrete blocks.
Space between wires in the fence —
its curls permanent,
not found in any beauty salon.
Space between gravel skirting sidewalks
and space between the grass blades
bordering the gravel and the damp space
in the dirt underneath. No purchase,

no perch for the wingless and naked,
he falls from the sky. Feathers so out of fashion.
Already there are so few birds.
The sky calls but the earth won't let go.

3

There is another world and he's spent years
looking for it, and in those years he's forgotten
the long list of this world even as it disappears.
Can't keep his shoes tied and now he's perfected
the public art of tying knots, uncertain
if a private art exists no matter how existential
his claims. He awakens to an alarm clock
marching to "The Star Spangled Banner"
and knows that patriotism is no substitute
for a cup of coffee. When he's finally ready,
he misses his target by years.

4

His watch band broke.
He wants to get it fixed.
Not a single store in town
with a replacement band.
The watch cost five dollars.
He starts carrying it around

in one of his pockets, but he keeps
forgetting which pair of pants
it's in: The ones hanging on the coatrack
or the ones belt-looped on a wall hook.
Time was in his pocket and he lost it.

5

Checking in, he empties his pockets:
cashier's receipt for weak gas-station coffee,
thumb-sized Swiss Army knife,
cell phone, metal detector gateway
to a naked underworld. In exchange,
he's given a playing-card-sized black box
with a long black ribbon, as if
a gift of mourning and not an alarm.
Driver's license held up to the glass,
the door buzzes open. How was Orpheus
able to recall his other life?

6

A ragged flight of women line up loosely across
the compound. Dressed the same, gray waist-length coats.
The right hand can't tell the difference from the left.
There are long days to discuss this. Towering poles bristle
with lights to watch over the guards, who watch over
the huddled flock, who watch over rumors of fox
and weasel. The lights aim in all directions.
Nothing is left unseen—no one's going
anywhere but here. Only the wind has wings.

7

In the group are two women
who killed their husbands. One in for fifteen years,
the other for life without parole for fifty years.
Another woman who planned
to be here isn't. She just went to solitary
for maybe a year carrying her allotment
of two books, one of them the requisite Bible.
Are we always alone ruined into knowledge
or is that too late too? Another woman,
refused release from a work detail,
turns back before she walks out the door,
"It's like the messiah's come
and I still have to work."

Knots

Hawk-wing wide, silver-sequined lapels soar
in the sunlight in front of the small crowd
each time The Great Manzini bends to select
a prop from the many spread over the single
plywood-sheet stage nailed to 2 X 6s.
He's inches above their sun-struck stares
and the vertigo of grass that sweeps to the horizon.

Boot-shaped sideburns kick his words
into the audience. Swept-back jet-black hair
rises a palm's width above his head, ready
to impersonate Elvis should the call come.
Extravagant gestures test the rope for strength,
integrity. His volunteer assistants wrap
his wrists and keep wrapping, commanded
to pull tight, then tighter, until the cord digs
into his skin. He feigns pain yet demands
tighter, followed by knots and more knots
until there is a gnarled pagoda crowning
his cinched wrists, his palms bound
as if in prayer as he walks into the audience
to confirm that his hands are not greased or oiled.
He begs for more knots from the children
who laugh and jostle in line, as if we don't
know that each knot is tied against the last
knot just like our lives.

The children love the tying, and the adults
are relieved that this knot is not tied
into their own histories of apologies, treaties
of forgiveness, broken-tongue-tied promises.

The Great Manzini returns to the stage,
hands above his head, feigns a few failed attempts,
and before anyone can be astonished, he's free
from nothing that would stop him from diving
into the grass for the Sirens sweet singing or drown
beside his car parked in another backwater day
on the gravel shoulder of a city park.

Meeting Frida Near the State Capitol

On the military post mid-century, I could go to movies
for a nickel and when I was finished with that life,
or thought I was finished, it was fifteen cents and a quarter
for the three-hour epics, *Sparticus, Lawrence of Arabia,*
Around the World in Eighty Days. During the week,
I walked the mile to the theater that was more a church
on a hill that rose up above an infinity of Kansas plains
off to the west, and on the opposite side of the parking lot
there was a church. In the darkness of the theater, after
black-and-white newsreels with their deep-throated commentaries
on the encroaching communist menace, the French defeat
at Dien Bien Phu, sputnik in a threatening orbit over our heads,
a solitary Japanese soldier still ready to die defending the atoll
he was abandoned on a dozen years after another war was retired,
I would see myself deep in someone else's story,
the poorly translated spaghetti westerns, the Roman legions
with lips out of sync with the dubbed dialogue, as if their lips
were clubbing the words I heard, oh, but the skeleton army
sown from the scattered teeth of some dead gorgon,
jumping out of the earth, shields and swords raised,
didn't need words. Then the British comedies with their agile
humor, it was a life robed in the dark, a sacrament of flickering
light, and now, four decades later, the sky a cold steel,
the parking lot a lake of iced asphalt, scattered with small islands
of stunted trees, the mall rises like a castle
with parapets of glass, and a dozen movie screens
crowded into one corner, where I buy a ticket from
a young woman, who turns and shouts to someone
in the back, "I sold one," then turns back
to me, "I hope you like weird movies."
The theater manager steps out to meet me

to explain, "It's kind of an artsy movie."
I say I don't mind. "Yes, but she's
a communist and bisexual." Robed in
darkness, finally, we meet alone.

In the Round
State Capitol Rotunda

We sit in one of many circles,
Each of us centered in his or her own
Widening circle even as we stay focused,

Centered. Circumference is our measure:
Vertical, horizontal, oblique, tangential.
Circularity spinning over, under, around us.

We spin and are spun together in circles—
concentricities we know and some
we don't know. Thoughts and desires

Circling a circular living:
Darkness to light to dusty darkness.
Within the roundness of these granite walls,

The circling stairs and balconies
Rising upward to a domed climax
Where the Roman goddess of harvest,

Motherly love, stands surveying
The city on a bluff as it spirals outward:
The river rippled round by a child's thrown stone,

The long meandering freight of coal and corn
Following the circuitous bottoms.
Bold in her sundown-bronzed vestments,

Ceres up from ancient roots, from the long story
Of our telling, namesake to the dwarf planet

Discovered between the orbits of Mars

And Jupiter, by a Sicilian monk, January 1, 1801,
Near Palermo. We harvest circles of light and time,
Energetic matters within the ever-expanding

Circumference of our curiosities. A celestial art,
A music of the spheres, hearing goddess and dwarf planet,
River and rotunda spiraling outward at once.

Hall of Waters

for Amy Beth Kirsten

He goes to the farthest stranger
who sits in the bow of a boat
moored to rotting wooden steps.

He stands beside water so dark
its bottom begins on the surface,
and in it the boat and stranger

are upside down and don't care
if they survive the flooding
sky or the cloudy river.

One branch, then another, is thrown
into the air that breaks into circles,
and then a stone sinks through both.

When asked from where he has come,
he remembers only his footprints
on this stretch of dirty sand.

When asked why, he says he owns
little and is owned by less,
and anyway he walked.

Small emissaries of thunder pass
and sickle-winged birds scar
the far bank with hoarse cries

as they lead the next generation
of rain south. Cottonwoods tremble

with pleasure and light.

The stranger invites him to
sit down in the blush of evening
but someone calls, reminding

him of time and how far he has
to go, and he turns to ask if this is
the way, and recalls the ocean broken

inside him. He leaves the stranger
whose boat is already carelessly
rocking out into the clouds.

2

The Whole Facts

Call it fact, mere fact, plain fact—
parts summed equal a whole
of some kind somewhere,
the sum no greater than itself,
so it's no longer true, facts
simply are. Pinto, Escort, Barracuda:
car parts are scattered deep across
the yard. Any whole is an accident.
Trace any accident back far enough
and it becomes inevitable.

The fact of this wind, stained with old
oil and simmering axle grease, rises out
of the hollow through unleafed
oaks and hickories, changes direction
and sweeps across the inevitable
accident that is me. I recall a baby's
startled gasp when rattle, bottle,
nipple didn't work, didn't satisfy,
and I blew into the plump crying face,
a warm breeze over the land of the wailing.
How the wide-eyed surprise was
accompanied by out-thrown arms
straight from a fat-diapered body,
as if in thanks or welcome back,
a startled embrace of the completely determined
accidental world.

Much like the Capa photograph
of a soldier downing a barren hill
during the Spanish Civil War,

his knees slightly buckled,
head turned aside from the lens,
as if he'd forgotten something
and embarrassed was about to turn
back, both his arms caught in that out-thrown
surprise, as if eighty years ago he'd been
hit by a bullet of breath and stopped
to lay down his rifle for a wide-eyed embrace
before he disappeared into scattered facts.

But in the wind that untangles itself
from the junk backed into this hollow,
the blooming dogwood leans over the porch,
floats its four-petalled pools of light
with a nervous elegance,
though each petal is notched and brown
at the edges, as if what's missing
was burned or shot away. Nearby
a blue jay scrapes at a scab of air,
others answer, and the sky is a clear
blue wound. A flock of warblers
migrates north across the yard
and field, flying low, just above
the rusting cars and bleached weed
stalks. A black cat leaps and swats one
bird out of the air. The flock flutters on,
a smaller whole, a winged army,
and for a moment, I grow calm
and remember what it means to grow whole
and smaller with each breath.

Dying of Strangers

A young girl sits down,
her scarred smile the only hint
of doubt. She has brought along
a photograph, a closeup of the deep
tooth tears, the hanging raw meat of self.

A dog must have thought, if a dog
thinks, as it tries to swallow
a voice, that it too can speak
of its loneliness, its hunger, or,
perhaps, it was simply chasing

something that disappeared into
her mouth and the dog was attempting
to save her at such a young age
from devouring her own death.
In living color, she holds the paper-thin

photo of loose slabs of cheek, lips hanging
with the sway of a rope bridge
across a chasm so deep the white-waved
river can't be heard, the little bobbing boats
of teeth capsizing on gummy red shoals.

Across her face, thin jagged
white lines radiate from
her mouth, as if the finest china
is forever spidering to pieces
at the dinner table of her face.

Rescuers

Let's see or not see, let's think or not think, but let's breathe
because we have no choice for the moment unless we're being
dragged through New Orleans in the petrochemical gumbo-gush
of Lake Pontchartrain, hearing a final time the gurgle of late night
saxophones and the lapping waves of applause as she teases off
her pasties and thong in submerged floodlights, crossing each new
night's gulf of unbridgeable sadness, as we spin past open doors
smoky with water, above the sidewalk canopies that cling to the sides
of buildings like sunken canoes, and catch for a moment a wrought-
iron lamppost with stiff arms, our bodies boarded closed, no longer
face up to the sky, no longer face down, except to those stranded
on rooftops who see us pass as they wave their arms at passing
helicopters, the whump-whump-whump of defeat and rescue, as we
perform our trick, floating above the street, slow motion superman
and woman. We didn't know that to gain superhuman powers we
had to hold our breath forever, never to be rescued.

Two to Four Weeks

for Terry Mitze

I'm sure I wasn't the one you wanted to talk to when you called,
but I was seated on the barstool in the kitchen by the cordless phone
under the glistening drops of wine glasses hanging from the ceiling
about to fall and break over the counter, when the phone rang
like any common solicitation or friend in need of a recipe,
and while everyone else was deeply animated in their many
   conversations
that spilled into the dining room and out the back door onto the lawn,
your name appeared in the visual display, and I wasn't thinking
or prepared to think that this could be the last time that these
   randomly
arranged numbers would appear wedded to your name,
and that from a certain perspective your name could be read
and still be a random arrangement of letters.

I answered; we began to talk, me trying to be upbeat, topical,
in the moment, avoiding what all of us had seen last July 4th,
frail and brittle, you claimed six months of the flu, none of us
believing it, none of us with enough courage to say anything
until after you left for your cross-country drive to California.
Now your voice weak, delicately urgent with what you want to tell me,
convince me, get me to accept, that there is nothing to worry over,
that you lived a full life, and at that moment, perhaps you were
   recalling
the Virgin Islands, the stray cat shot through the eye and dead
on the porch on your first Caribbean morning, a tarantula nailed
to the front door, and the taillights of your newly bought used car
   gouged out,
or in Tanzania jumping in a circle on a cold morning with the red-
   robed Masai,

running out the back door to catch a bus as gunfire erupted
in the sweltering streets of Nyakabindi.

I lamely assured you that we are each other's time out of time,
that you will always be a part of the July 4th party conversations,
or any other time, that we wouldn't hesitate to make you the butt of
        our jokes,
though what kind of joke is it when last July erupted around us,
a momentary glitter and bang of white-whistling chrysanthemums
and the soaring stab of shooting stars pulled from gold and silver
        scabbards,
then our fading back into the dark, into bodiless voices punctuated
by the occasional mosquito slap and the next sputtering fuse.

 It was then that you discussed your plan to retire early, maybe one
        more year
of work, that you planned to cash in whatever it was that you had to
        cash in,
your liquid assets to flow freely in all directions till the end,
as if you knew the closeness of that end, but not the depth of the
        closing.
Later, hot, humid, for the beginning of autumn, hindered by the
        usual
complications all sweating to be noticed, addressed, resolved,
        dissolved,
oaks clutching their leaves as the great turning away begins, a flush
        of red
and then the long clear outline of winter—I wasn't the one and then
        I was
as you put down the phone.

Overdose

1 Flight

The teenager who pulls lightly on
her lashes, lifting her eyelids
just enough to place two paper-thin
dots saturated with God's windowpane—
I wish she was here, right now, to see
the bowed heads, how hardly anyone
bothers to look up from their newspapers,
the pages prayers turning quietly as their breathing.
In upper atmospheric turbulence, they retreat
from the headlines into the narrowest
certainties of their belted seats. Deep in
the belly of habit and routine, so out of
proportion to the scale of their circumstance,
floating among clouds and mountains,
they fall out of the air toward the airport.

2 Hotel

She could be here, right now, listening
from this third floor balcony to the shouts
rising from the sand court, to see how
the volleyball floats then falls unattended,
then rises languorously again, as if seated
on a pedestal of air. Against the hard blue
sky, the ball is another slip of paper she slips
under her eyelids, and written through
the air are the little miracles she hoped
to read so clearly in the hours between
hours that it takes for the white wafer
to fall back into the hands of the players
as they volley up their lives.

3 Mall

With both hands on the restaurant's
wooden fence, meant to separate diners
from strollers, she jumps over and back,
as if she were trying to meet her own
rippling revisions. Unable to decide
whether to be carried along by the crowd
or sit down at the cramped table to eat,
she's immersed in the cry and clamor.
Her arms wave at all who walk by
embracing the softening light of anonymity,
ready to sing and perch on the graceful
anthem of evening, to declare this day hers
as her eyelids dissolve into air.

Where Hieronymus Washes His Hands

A stifling stench sizzles
the shovel's flat blade.
At the bottom of another hour,

burning creosote. All hours are one,
hobbled and drudging
through a fuming lust.

Tramped, cramped, bent, and staring
through the chimney's clean-out door,
the bucket beside him heaped full, smoke

begins to choke the room from the ceiling
down. The pall stops knee-high,
held up by the flat muscle of cold

that crawls through the open front door.
Through a smoldering haze, the slant shadows
of chairs and table legs give body

to the tilted air. He steps out of the house,
off the porch, smoke and steam clinging
to his night clothes and the path he follows.

With a flashlight, he swats the stars
swarming over the field. An instant
madness of ashen ends.

He fills the bucket with water
from the creek. A black churning
hisses and strikes, scalding his hands.

He drops the bucket spewing cinders.
The charred tongue of fire
quickens the hard-hearing earth.

Apocalyptic Godiva

It happens, the weather changes,
there's a depression in the bed surrounded
by a storm of sheets and blankets.
The bruised tower of pillows,

linen cumulus at one end of the mattress.
The headboard stretches to the horizon
that won't go away and can't be reached.
From all sides, walls of pastel fog press in.

She lies there forecasting faces.
She will do what's necessary, panic, call for help,
then panic more. From her angle, staring
over the edge, the floor is her ceiling.

She can't raise her hand to wave, move
her head toward the phone's luminous face.
With one foot free, with her big toe, she reaches
the nightstand to punch speed dial.

The police break the deadbolt, unhinge
the locked bedroom door. The paramedics find her,
stroke victim who woke twisted as a bolt
of lightning. They hear the whimpering,

hungry dog curled in the debris of the kitchen.
Steel-stethoscope moons swing
from the medics' necks. They can't lift
or roll her. They scissor away her gown.

She's free to stand, naked and shivering.
No stroke of luck to weather the sweet tooth
of loneliness: Mars, Butterfingers,
Mounds, Twix, unwrapped, half-eaten,

rolled in the sheets, melted against her body,
then hardened in the cold of an unheated apartment.
No downpour, quake, force-ten gale to shake her
free of this sweet apocalypse.

Errancy

What was I to tell him
when he showed up on my doorstep,
his armor stained with rust
and covered with mildew,
that he arrived too late,
that the country of wounded windmills
had sailed an ocean and transformed
a singular sorrowful countenance
into giants of industry from sea to shining sea,
from oil-slick-rainbowed rivers
to majestic museums honoring extinction,
that his ancient nag was no match
for a Hummer even if he fattened it
on fast food, that his campaign
of evils to undo, wrongs to right,
injustices to correct, abuses to ameliorate,
and offenses to rectify couldn't survive
the howlers of hate radio and reality TV,
that he'd never get elected?

He said my next-door neighbors
thought he was a lunatic,
the house across the street
saw him as an impractical dreamer,
that he too readily spoke to himself
scared most everyone,
and no one stalled in traffic at the intersection
would wind down their car window
as he stood with a pail of dirty water
scooped from the median fountain,
balanced on the saddle of a skinny swayback horse,

his lance raised and ready with a skewered squeegee,
so poverty pursues him relentlessly,
as he gallops across this desiccated plain
of millionaires and the homeless.

It didn't help that his sidekick, Sancho,
had scraped his knees raw
trying to slow him down,
his fat palms swollen fatter from so many
heartrending prayers on his master's behalf.
But really what's left for any of us,
knighted and benighted each Friday midnight
at the Thirsty Turtle and Gladstone Bar & Grill,
and later retreating behind closed doors,
lost in the grandeur of our delusions,
quixotically charging ahead into the next room
where night's blued armor might hide us
while we sleep it off, if we ever can.

In Her Own Flight

He saw her leave the ground once.
He wanted to brush his hands
under the soft soles of her feet.

He wanted to be the magician
controlling the illusion.
The audience waiting for his hands

to lead their eyes into flight.
She knows all his tricks.
She will never give him credit

for her own aerial astonishment.
Still he thinks, it would be nice
to have empirical evidence.

Only he needs proof, she thinks,
knowing the burden that is lifted,
when she reaches for the Carolina

parakeets, Amelia Earhart, the Graf
Zeppelin. She never doubts
the air she stands on.

Does it matter he never saw her
land? He wonders, if she never lands
has she ever flown? Does air

then become solid and familiar
as ground? He tries to describe
her wings. Maybe it's the blur

in the corner of his eye. Maybe
it's her arms folded quiet as wings.
How easily she would fall,

if this were ordinary flight
where flying means falling
into feathered hands.

Point of No Returns

I want to introduce you as a friend.
No, not a friend, though we could be
friends at the right hour of the day
some week of the year. If anything,
we acknowledge heading in a direction,

if only toward the door closing in our faces,
our voices passing into distances
absorbed by the street. It would serve
neither of us to say acquaintance,
as though we are no more than stray

collisions, propelled and repelled
by each other's presence, that neither
of us are quick enough to get out
of the other's way. So please, let me
introduce you and not mention the point

that there was no point in us
ever knowing why we were not lovers,
and will always be doubtful lovers;
just as the man who steps out
of the Sears Building feels an updraft

of Chicago heat and knows in all
his doubt the city continues to burn
a century later; just as the woman
feels the quake of waves resonate
up through the waterlogged pilings

of Fisherman's Wharf, doubts that

these coastal hills will stop shaking her
off the map; just as the pilot, who reaches
the point-of-no-return, continues, fuel
too low to turn back and too low to arrive.

Hagiography of Faults

Backed against
the windows fall
floats, inflates,
of its own burning.
hard against walls.
a holding action
the rising shoals
On the porch,
breath,
into my face.
a devastating
No chance
an angel.
I answer
fracturing

so much dark
away. The house
on the light
Shadows lean
This is retreat,
 against the sirens,
of a hardened night.
strata of cold repel
shove it back
Stars drop
distance.
of ever catching
Saved by a ringing,
to a smaller
slippage.

No, I felt nothing.
I turn to see
is swinging,
asleep undisturbed
another
under the wood-
by the heat.
no door slammed,
silent in cabinets.
the dog refused
for its evening walk.
hanging over
a wild pendulum,
the whole house

Am I sure?
if the pull chain
if there's a cat
on the couch,
on the floor
stove, blanked
Not one hinge creaked,
dishes remained
Earlier
to go out
She says the light
her kitchen table was
that every pane shivered,
suffered a nervous breakdown.

A mule and mile
not profane tremor,
of holy quaking.
rivers are baptizing
pealing a thousand
christening a new
Regardless
cities are
everlasting rubble.
if my life tilted,
but I said, the dog

apart and I felt nothing,
not a moment
She is convinced
backwards, church bells
miles away,
saint's day.
of the hour,
knee-deep in
She is convinced
I wouldn't notice,
refused a rainy walk.

Ghost Technology

I haven't taken a photograph where you didn't appear
in color after three days in the poorly alphabetized
racks of others' family vacations, birthday parties,
holiday reunions, appearing within the white

borders of discounted developing for all
to see all. Looking closer at what I'm holding
in my hands, it's a blurred image of you trying
to escape the maniacal glass eye and its single
syllable shutter that sends with each click

a flutter through your body, as if you were
pictured flying from inside out. Hand held up
to the lens, face turning away, only completes
the flawed flourish of a gesture. The ratcheting
whine and wind of film, too personal a theft,

something that should remain wrapped
in your sinew, clinging to your bone.
The camera a pick-pocketed perfection,
leaving you filmed, pressed into two
hand-sized dimensions, a life lived,

not a living. Perhaps that's what troubles
you, in such a hurry to arrive at the end,
these photographic fragments, a record
of timing, slowing your headlong progress,
and even a blur or simply out of focus,

over or underexposed, is not enough,
or is it still too much. Your desire for the unframed

life: the photograph of a living room,
the window blinding against the shadowed
wall, couch burning with sunlight, a book

open on the coffee table to a blank page,
a clear-glass vase, nearly invisible, holding
the woody vein of a long stemmed flower,
petals beginning to droop, a haunting
remembrance, you beyond the borders.

Naked History

Even exhaustion cries out for more.
Then naked abstractions crowd the bedroom.
Hard hours to sort out the historical
From the anecdotal.
Was it only the wallpaper?
One wall of ancient Athenian ships mounted
with battering rams
headed for splintery penetrations.
The next wall covered
with ships' shattered hulls, sails afire,
the motion of men and swords
painted still as the swarms of arrows suspended in flight.
The third wall blurred
by the finest curtains of silk smoke
as ships sink and men float
in the centers of their own crimson bouquets,
a blackened sail blooms over the water,
a mast's stem a final exclamation
barely clearing the choppy surface.
Around the next inside corner,
the settling waves gather up
the remaining ships,
a few men hoisted out of the waters,
the mangled left to the hungry sea,
and beyond, the long curve of horizon
obsessively alone.
The fifth wall blank,
flat white,
where the cries of muscled men
are still heard,
below the grief of all the ecstasies
that were once theirs.

Blouse

Distasteful discourse, diatribe, disquisition, over lunch, but not
The lunch, and not a simple faux pas, not a sleight slight and not

Of hand, more a felony and now it lies crumpled,
Abandoned of body in the laundry basket, waiting

To be cleansed of claims, accusations, censure.
This pariah of apparel, this stake through

The heart of sensibility, this fashion failure,
That she cut out on the brick floor,

A geography of flattened felt, one-dimensional Tlingit
Vision of the animal spirit. The continents of back

And front, the peninsulas of sleeves,
The thin atoll of collar, to be sewn together,

seamstress sewing Gondwanaland back together
After a hundred million years, or Mary Shelley

Stitching the chapters of a lonely woman together.
It's a blouse, the sewing machine whirring

Like a hive of excited bees, the sting of its creation
Yet to come. The fabric a muted pink,

A lightly flushed orange, patterned with white
dime-sized cats in groups of six and nine,

Mostly in profile with red or green bows,

Each cat coven encircling a stringed balloon,

Premonition of coming clawed critics.
The fourteen to forty crowd who spill midriffs

And cinch bulging thighs with zippered denim,
Unable to contain themselves, no matter

The material, the cat out of the bag,
Their dislike, disdain, disturbingly

Uncivilized for a blouse bewildered
By a modicum of baggy modesty.

What Happens to Such People

One day the little red lamps of columbines swing in the wind,
a light the hummingbirds find and drink.
The blue jay in the bushes is startled
by the ground and is swallowed by its own harsh voice.

One day the sky is a blue halo around each leaf,
a luminous shimmer. It's sent off into summer's
green pavilions without a return address.

One day a phoebe builds a nest
on top of the light by the door. We astonish
each other as I turn the corner
and we fly in opposite directions.

One day on the porch, sleeves of sun rest
in the aluminum chair. I never learned
to say no, therefore never learned to say yes.

I look for wasps in the legs of pants
hung on the clothesline. I take them down
and know the sting of one day,
pants that can't come off fast enough.

Domino Coffee Shop

. . . the vacant into the vacant
The captains, the merchant bankers . . .
—"East Coker," T. S. Eliot

His wife, the astrologer, the diviner of all
confused tendencies, stargazer and planet
reader, knows that Saturn returns every ten
years to club us over the head, kick us in
the groin, encourage us to divorce spouses,
run off to other cities with the kids to live
with gay men, and that's what she does.

Second, and in the same year, his brother
dies. He flies to Seattle, closing his coffee
shop for a week, trusting that his help would
drink up the profits, offer unlimited free
refills, flood the sidewalk with a foaming
elixir. He returns to a sympathetic
and disgruntled clientele. He read a selection
from Four Quartets at the funeral.

Third, and the year isn't over yet,
his father dies, and he flies back to Seattle.
He closes his shop again. His customers
are beginning to doubt his veracity; how
could so much happen to one person
in a single year. Caffeine withdrawal
cuts into his business. Dressed in his
only suit he continues to read Eliot.

The year has no end, or so
he begins to believe when he loses

his business, having forgotten to sign
the lease, yet continuing to pay his bills,
but the competition up the street wants
to open a second business and closes the deal.
Out on the street, filling the back
of his decade-old car with chairs and tables,
he's litigating antitrust, not to mention suing
for his espresso maker's water pump, burned up
by the landlord shutting off the water to hurry him out.

If in his beginning is his end, he wants
to know why this year doesn't know that—
his apartment burns down, the furnace
caught fire, and the landlord, money launderer
and suspected drug dealer, shows up with
two policemen. The one dressed in black
combat fatigues tells him that it's a well kept
secret that the constitution doesn't guarantee
any right to privacy, his hand on his revolver
during the entire discourse. He wonders
if these are the "hollow men."

Sixth, if not a new year then a new city,
time/space an uninterrupted continuum,
and he's the domino of disaster falling
that far and farther; he's told a realtor he'll
rent the apartment on the West End,
but he doesn't have the money, and the car
he's driving, overloaded with tables and chairs,
riding on the axles, leaves the streets brimming
with the aroma of burning clutch as he pulls away.

Trouble Behind Glass Doors

With apologies to Kenneth Patchen and the Journal of Albion Mooonlight

for Bobette

We drove past once or twice the last year.
            The house now gone a decade.
     We wondered
who lived there,
             what happened, where did they go—though
we really wondered about us.

                  The windows cracked
and broken. Socketed shadows gaped before the dust rising
around our feet.
            The porch settled, sagged—its weathered
                     floor sinking,
thin wooden columns hanging
                   from the roof,
the world less than solid, nailed to this sky
as it hurtled into rot and space.

                  The porch swing
swung from one chain spilling
        nights drenched in humid air.
The other chain snagged on a sickle moon.
Trumpet vines
              once brushed the backs of our necks
at the zenith of the creaking arc.
               A shroud of honeysuckle
entangled the trellis, fattened the air with its fragrance.

Before its final razing, the house had no sense
                of modesty left,

nothing hidden or secreted, all was loss and lost,
simply waiting to tumble
                    from the uncloseable front door.
                                        Inside,
we were repulsed by neglect.
                              The crumbling plaster drew us in,
sifted down from the ceiling onto the floor.
Mouse-shredded carpet littered the corners.
                                        In the kitchen
no trace of the scorpion that once crawled
from under a cabinet. No trace of the pot-bellied stove
that consumed whole trees yet kept
                                    no one warm. Face-high
on the north bedroom wall, the fist-sized
                                        hole teemed
with wasps' coming and going.

                              ⋯ ≣✦≣ ⋯

Found, forty years
                    bookmarked,
the handmade envelope, yellowed as evening
                                        stretched to breaking,
a late light that catches clouds of August
                              insects rising over the growing
shadows of unmowed fields.
                              One corner of the tape that sealed
the letter,
              is folded over. Frail, it sticks
to the page of a book that reads:

The question is not: do we believe in God?
but rather: does God believe in us?

Creased once, opening brittle as wasp wings left on the sill
between storm windows,
                    the perse-edged paper bears
lines fine as a brushed
                          single camel hair,
          bearing words so
        delicate they bend under the pressure of reading,
words that long to return to their own year.

         What's done, what's left to do? There's so much
we didn't imagine.
         The letter can't be delivered,
can't be returned. There's an oak's
               shadow edging slowly
past a quince bush, where goats once foundered
              on afternoon visions
of morning-glory seeds. Forty years later,
the letter ends: What is here is
           elsewhere. What is not here
is everywhere. There is only
       one of us.

               ✦

There is nothing to deliver or remove—
         I have no letter, no dog-eared scrap of paper,
the address no more than Fifth Street
           between Elm

and Locust–the numbered streets running
north-south, the trees east-west.

                The slope of the hill
seems right
        though I can't remember the sun
streaking a single shadow across any space of that year.

                    Perhaps the rooms
had fallen into the silence
           of spiders.
I must have lived in the shadows of those months,
            framed by daily longing
and war and smaller wants.

        The attic stairs,
              railingless and steep,
as if the house needed a way to enter another dimension quickly,
      led up to a single room, whose walls,
ceiling, roof were one and the same,
           and at either gable
a small window painted shut.
              Standing in the middle
of that room was the promise
        of a condemned house.
              Written in black on
the dim east wall:
. . . only an unbeliever could have created our image
        of God; and only a false God could be satisfied . . .

Why was I still there?

We never leave the places

                    we've lived.

We construct and reconstruct our absences.

                                   The address of

our disbeliefs written on the back of napkins,

        lost at the bottom of pockets and purses.

3

Tolstoy's Ants

What is it all but a trouble of ants
In the gleam of a million million of suns?
—Tennyson ("Vastness," 1889)

Monday a record snowfall for March. Boot high
And deeper. Cars found themselves parked in ditches.
Tuesday it's in a race to melt and take the hillside with it.
The creeks climb over themselves with everywhere to go.
Wednesday the counter is covered with ants.
Shouting does no good. Their long lines can't hear
Over the dark rhythm they possess. It's a losing
Proposition believing there's any chance
For negotiations. Door or poison, that's it.
It's unconditional surrender, nothing less.
Sure, stop feeding the cat on the counter
By the sink, but there's always a forgotten bowl
Waiting to be washed or some crumb that tumbled
From the table. Crawling across the floor,
The tiny minions keep rewriting their one long
Sentence back into the history of a queen's care.
They form a dark jumbled wreath around the clear
Drops. Still it's not enough, and next day the hordes
Descend again, preparing to punctuate
War and Peace across cold linoleum floor.

In These Times

It was not her intention, sitting quietly,
hands nested in her lap,
holding themselves for comfort,
to convince herself of her wholeness.
Eyes closed wanting only to listen,
to be reduced to pure vibration,
a quivering inner ear like the picture
of her uncle, standing defiantly crazed
on sagging sandbags, wearing
a looping necklace of ears
to better hear the multitudes.

She recalls that first hint of breeze
after days of unapologetic heat,
that moment the lilac leaves imperceptibly
shivered and the honeysuckle scent
began to drift across the porch,
she at the edge of a fragrant listening.

Eyes open to confirm that she'd not fallen
from the chair, but caught there at a loss
for giving any kind of directions
on how to find her, hostage
to that other moment, yet still sitting
next to a young man who believes
that she is sitting there,
even as her face fades.

Her coat draped over
the chair, a wounded soldier
folded into grief, a soul

waiting to be rescued, waiting
for one arm, then the other
to be slipped into a sleeve,
then to button the body closed.

Neighbors

—for Rezak

When a neighbor shows up at his door
Wearing a black ski mask, carrying something large
And automatic, aiming at his every move,
Refusing to speak, using only the rough motion of hands,
Indicating whatever he wants and that he
must do exactly what the neighbor wants him to do,
Without hesitations, no questions, this is a new life.

When he's marched onto the front porch,
Hands above his head, as if he's already reaching
For heaven, then down the few steps
To the newspaper-sized lawn, to stand,
He sees other men in similar positions surrounded
By their armed, ski-masked neighbors,
This is their new lives too.

When he's forced onto a school bus, forced
Into silence, forced to witness
The man seated next to him already
Flying the red banners of his inner life
In this absurd parade led by neighbors,
The windows taped shut, the heaters
Turned full-blast, this is their lives in a long line
Of busses headed for summer camp.

When they are driven through the empty streets
Beyond the city limits and stop in front
Of a series of drab company buildings,
they are unloaded with their arms folded
Over their heads, and in a half-crouch, stumble
Through a gauntlet of cursing, spitting,
Kicking neighbors, this then is their old lives come back.

When in a room so crowded with horror,
Where they sleep standing shoulder to shoulder,
Through a crack in the shed wall he sees
Neighbors strip a neighbor with long hunting knives
Then cut off a pound of flesh, his debt so great,
And, as he bleeds away, the body doused
with gasoline, this man's life and his own are aflame.

When he wanted to deny the name called
From the guarded door, a name that had grown
Heavier each day until he wanted nothing
To do with it, as if there was a choice,
As if growing lighter was a new solution,
As he ate his one slice of daily bread,
All he could do is step forward.

When he knew how many had not returned
For roll call after the first day and all the days
That followed, he turned to the room of starving faces
And said he'd be back, but they did not expect much,
Hope plucked of its feathers,
Boiled in a pot and the thin gruel drunk dry.

When there is not a gram of body fat to cushion
The blows that break ribs and teeth,
There is only time to stop it from happening
All at once. If he's lucky, whatever he is this day,
He is what is missing, and waits for the neighbors
to discover what's left of his other life.

Paperwork

...in the smell of apples at the close of day...
—Czesław Miłosz

Papers scattered on the desk,
rising from the floor, occupying chairs,
kitchen table, countertops—
yellowed notes of an untranscribed life:

    stubby woodcock,
unperturbed, crossing a snow-covered
February back road, undone
by a late-winter storm, plump belly
plowing along, its slow pumping gate
clownish, following the overly long beak
of a landlocked, land-loving shorebird;

    words yet to find sentences: Ophidian,
stygian, millefleur, paranomasia, Parousia, parsec,
paroxysm;

    movies to see: *Why Has Bodhi-dharma
Left For the East, Latcho Drom, Gleaners
and I;*

    quotes from here and there:
If you stick your head in a mortar,
it does no good to fear the sound
of the pestle, Destiny caresses a few
and molests others;

    sweet red peppers,
eggplant, brown eggs, sage, fresh basil,

grocery lists too old to eat;

what must be done
yesterday and the day before, today too full:
vacuuming, mopping, bills paid,
bills to pay, threats of repo, rejection;

the endless pleas:
whales, wolves, wolverines, weasels,
water, world;

letters I meant to answer,
distant friends I've kept waiting, searching
for what I should have said long ago;
not finding what I once remembered,
but armfuls of loose papers
falling into time's other country,

not unlike
late morning March 16th, 1988, Halabja,
clouds of dust kissing dust,
the heat rising to noon, the sky clear,
the whomp, whomp, whomp,
of a helicopter leaving footprints across
the city sky, stomping the tops of houses,
refining the rubble as soldiers lean
out the side doors—

there are those who say
they tossed prayer flags or confetti
or the severed wings of white doves,

the white wish of peace floating down the air,
white lilies, white lies with longer shadows—

    no, it was just paper,
maybe newspaper with old news
of the old dead, the dying, the living
doing it again, maybe shredded memos
and accounts from the bureaus of a Byzantine
bureaucracy, maybe pages of books torn
from ancient stacks, read a last time
by scared birds, flocks of paper
winging the air, gliding on the secret
shiftings of the invisible,

    before the noon currents
drove families into cellars
where they inhaled the odor of sweet apples—
it was spring,

    leaves withered,
birds fell from trees, goats reared
and collapsed, midday knee-high fog
smothered the desert streets,

    eyes burned to blindness
with all this paper work
to be completed.

El Playón
San Salvador, 1983

If someone should disappear,
                    a friend, a father,
you might take a deep breath
                            before walking the road
beyond the city limits,
                    past the haunted hours of worry,
the dirt-floor houses
                where chickens roost on window sills,
where the family sow
                    sprawls across the porch
beside empty crates.

Walk past the charred stumps,
                    the exhausted fields:
sweet potatoes, beans, soil
                            washed into the river.
Past even the living trees
                    filled with parrots' alarms
of red and blue, and their stricken cries,
                            to where the road hardens
on the side of a volcano then ends.
                    There they may be found resting
in awkward stiffened postures
                    as if a door opened
                            on lovers who shield
only their eyes from strangers
                    and the circling vultures,
the wandering pigs.
                    To them all flesh

is equal, not understanding
　　　　how we cherish a finger
that touched deeply,
　　　　　　lips that moved beyond speech.

The random syllables of their names
　　　　　　　wind-whipped over the edges
of ancient lava and trucked-in refuse,
　　　　　　as if they were still headed for the late shift
at the shirt factory,
　　　　　　pushing a wheelbarrow,
borrowing a cup of sugar,
　　　　　　and for you they are
not here
　　　　　　laid out and broken,
　　　　　　　　stripped of the world.

War Feathers

My father somewhere in the Korean War.
My mother and I outside Cincinnati
living in a trailer. I have a black
and white photo of him beside the lamp
next to my bed. He's dressed in dusty fatigues,
the pockets of his baggy pants, I think
filled with air, as if he were about to rise
off the frozen ground and be blown away,
but that wouldn't happen for another thirty years.
He's posing, his body slightly turned, his arm raised,
elbow bent so his hand is level with his shoulder,
as he holds the polished metal of a .45.

Was it the same year I lay in bed with food poisoning?
How suffering bookmarks a year. That summer
I was playing Go Fish with my grandfather.
He and my great-grandfather always cheated,
one looking over my shoulder, signaling to the other
what card not to choose. Mad, I stormed off
the porch and ran across Virginia Avenue,
looking up at the telephone lines, anxious, waiting
for a call from a bullet-proof father to rescue me.

Perched on the black looping line a twittering banana
peel, no, a singing drop of gold, no, a bird,
and when I ran to tell my grandparents, they didn't
believe me, but persistence brought them
to the front yard, where they took off their hats
and began throwing them at the bird, hoping
to frighten it down. Anyone who drove past,
seeing two old men throwing their fedoras high
into the air, would have thought them celebrating,
perhaps a son or grandson still alive, home early.

North Ninth Street

Not time, nor place
Did then adhere.

—Lady Macbeth

Many streets like this one,
but only this one in this town,
and every day at five o'clock
a modestly dressed man, the same
man each afternoon, one who would
dress no other way but modestly,
walks out of the just-locked bank doors
between the façades of Corinthian columns,
turns the corner of the building to reach
this street where he removes
three green metal boxes
stenciled with the bank's name,
that rest during bank hours over the faces
of three parking meters,
hoods over the condemned
awaiting curbside executions
or monks deep in meditation
on the day's slippage as shadows
cross the street not caring
how many times they are listed
in the police blotter as hit and run,
time contained in these box-blind spaces
that clank in his hands as he returns
to unlock the empire's double glass doors.

And a young clerk, aproned and energetic,
thinking of some evening event
to draw her back into this life,
steps out of a flower shop into the frame

of late light, where she looks up and down
this one street, at the potted plants sunning
along the sidewalk below the storefront
window, and begins to carry them inside,
one hand gripping the clay pot's lip,
the other firmly around the braided trunk,
so a ficus tree strolls past ferns,
miniature rose bushes, and rustles
leisurely through the door,
the street display defoliated by quitting time,
though the rumpled man enthroned
on the bench, his life's possessions
scattered like collapsed parachutes at his feet,
sorts for a final accounting before landing
beside a dumpster or alley for the night,
Agent Orange and Birnam Wood one.

Oh Say Can You See

She broke her foot at a 40th anniversary Woodstock party
held eighteen hundred miles as the crow flies from Yasgur's farm.
Fifth metatarsal on her left foot, same as her father,

only he dragged his plaster cast through the roar of Vietnam,
while The Who bashed out "My Generation" to a half-million kids
in 1969, as Peter Townsend batted Abbie Hoffman, annoying fool

and jester, off the stage with his guitar. The rain kept coming.
The floodlights' wet tracers targeting the shivering
naked bodies huddled under shreds of plastic,

but they all survived, even the brown acid, except one young man
who slept-in the middle of a farm road and was passed over
by a dual-wheeled John Deere. The mud ankle deep as a rice paddy,

but the music kept blasting. On a blacked-out Saturday night,
really early Sunday morning, not alert to ambush,
she caught her sandal in a cracked asphalt driveway.

Hendrix' pain still spangling the stars through speakers
balanced in the windows. She was carried
off in a psychedelic-strobed ambulance, her father

under the thumping beat of helicopter blades
and the counterpoint of cover fire. Like father,
like daughter, succumbing to the next step and the next.

Foreign Policy

Stan Laurel, Oliver Hardy,
Stan Hardy, Oliver Laurel,
inseparable, impeccable, in their scratchy
black & white century-old moving
silence. They stop at the beginnings
of the Southern California suburbs.
Christmas, the weather balmy,
demanding little: light coats,
bowler hats. The sky held up
by the arching trunks of transplanted palms
and their wide huckster smiles.
They step out of their Model T,
knock on the door of a stuccoed house.
A tree is not needed. They carry
the four-feet-tall pine to the next house.
A man answers, says no, irritated
to be solicited on Christmas,
slams the door in their faces, catches
the edge of Laurel's coat in the jamb.
Hardy rings the door bell,
the door opens, he's not quick enough
to draw back before the door slams again,
the new home owner more aggravated than ever.
Ring slam. Ring slam. That's the routine.
Then a limb of their Christmas tree is caught
and Hardy begins to dismantle the door.
The man storms out of the house,
begins tearing off the car's bug-eyed headlights,
doors, and seats. The two itinerant salesmen watch
in disbelief as the chaos of parts piles up.
Laurel and Hardy turn their attention

to the house, breaking windows,
ripping out the phone,
breaking the door into kindling.
The homeowner stares
at his house being demolished.
A crowd gathers on the sidewalk,
astonished at this mutual destruction.
Furniture piled in the yard
is hosed down. Each time
the offended turn back
more dedicated to destroying
the other. Car, house.
House, car. Offense, insult.
Insult, offense. The police arrive.
sporting billy clubs, talking to the crowd,
they don't know what to do.
Laurel and Hardy drive off
in a steel skeleton, happy
to have escaped, believing
their cause just. The home owner,
arms crossed, satisfied, amid the debris.

Derailed

I

Cottonmouths, alligator snappers, hellbenders,
frogs, clouds of mosquitoes until the swamps
were drained, the cypress clear-cut,
their arthritic roots upended and burned.
Tracks laid to carry out timber.
Plumes of coal smoke, glistening backs
of sweating stokers, glowing cinders
falling on the gravel beds between oak
ties—fire's work, and nothing
to celebrate but being on time. In farmhouses
and towns beside the tracks, the days divided
by the moan of warning whistles. The valleys
of August 14, 1902, thick with humidity
and faces crammed into windows coming up
for breath, as the Iron Mountain train
worked its way from the south out of a stifling heat.
No. 4 northbound pulled to a sidetrack to let
the No. 1 pass, headed for Little Rock.
No. 4 late for St. Louis, crossed the trestle
over Big River. A hardscrabble farmer
waited to step the ties that made a hundred
little bridges for the steel rails. At seventy,
a veteran, he lived off his Civil War pension
and once crossed greater dangers
than a timbered bridge. He's stopped
by something he hasn't heard in years, a muffled cry.
Near the gorge's edge, a dented valise
that fell from the train. He opens it cautiously.
Inside a baby wearing knit shirt, flannel
skirt, a wool scarf with ten small black

pyramids pulled tight over its face. The baby blue
from lack of air. For the first few years, unidentified
women came, sometimes spoke, sometimes not,
as if all mothers had thrown at least one
broken heart into the arms of a stranger.

2

Headlines read, *Iron Mountain Baby*
Born of Locomotive and Mountain,
but the child, grown now, didn't want
anyone to know that he missed
the gorge and falling into Big River.
Rather a rock ledge dented his skull, leaving
his head swollen for days, and maybe that's why,
years later, he favored his left leg, and his left arm
always moved a little stiffly. His worst
nightmare was being unable to open a suitcase.
Was his mother the woman dressed in black
who showed up five days after the newspapers
featured his rescue by the old farmer?
She walked in the front door of the cabin,
held his small body, kissed him, and left without
speaking, leaving ten dollars. He can't remember,
but the story of pregnant and unwed, the train
whistle blowing as it crossed the bridge when she shoved
the valise out the window, is what he thinks he knows.
Was it his second birth so soon after the first, out of
the heavy, steady panting of a locomotive, that later,
without warning, not mentioning a word to friends,

leaving a half-finished article for his newspaper,
mail unopened on his desk, and hearing a whistle
stretch across fields and towns, that led him to abandon
his office, his home, his family, not to be heard
from again, assuming a different name,
to be derailed in another life?

Games

—For Bob Dyer and Tom Cassidy

Dead in the Denver airport restroom,
wallet crammed with thousand dollar bills.
A drug deal gone beyond bad. No claims on the body.

One night, years before, a campesino's cow wandered
onto the road just out of sight over a hill—
he paid extravagantly for the crushed fender.

Cheaper and quicker than bribing the Federales,
and probably saved him from disappearing forever,
though he only postponed forever a few years.

At the ruins of Chichén Itzá, he lay in the moon-choked grass
of the ball court before guards kept tourists confined
to daylight. He loosened a block from the wall

belonging to the House of the Dead; every stone a carved
limestone skull. He carried it under the spare in the trunk
as he crossed the Rio Grande. Perhaps because the car

was damaged, the border guards didn't search it, believing
he had enough troubles. He left the grinning stone
at a friend's house; his transient life unable to bear

the weight. Years after his death, his friend decided
to return the stone. Because it was not officially removed,
officially on loan, no stone was officially missing

from the wall of death, so could not be returned,
officially or unofficially. Offered to a museum,

it lacked provenance, proof of purchase,

proof of customs, proof of transport, proof that it
belongs anywhere. Officially denied, a vagrant death
waits, grinning at itself in the mantel mirror.

Give or Take a Day or Two

I

All the flags flying, May 21, 2011, and if they're not,
well, who cares? Harold Camping certain beyond
certain: sell the house, quit the job. Countries, oaths,
allegiances—gone, or soon to be gone. The daily tattered,
the weekly ravaged, what's left and all around.
Maybe there's enough flag-gallant yardage
to wrap a body or two, going naked unanticipated
by people who've spent their lives trying to keep it
under wraps, tied up, chained in their pants,
the public exposure a traumatic rapture.

People so worried they're praying
like there's no tomorrow.
Isn't that the point and half the joke.
Scattered all along the street, piles of free clothes
for the 99%, maybe even wallets, new identities,
cash, windfall credit, though heavenly sums
are out of the question. And the cars,
don't forget the shiny cars, at least the ones
suddenly driverless that haven't smashed head-on
into trees, telephone poles, or flipped over guardrails,
but the rest, in parking lots, their engines still running,
welcoming new drivers to open the door,
take possession from God's abandoned used-car lot.
Just toss the shoes left by the accelerator out the window,
push aside the shirt with its paisley tie
still tucked under the collar, but that's wishful thinking,
and the other half of the joke that's the next day.

2
February 6, 1925

I tell you it's coming. We are people of the book
and the book reveals to us our end, and we are ending
according to German-born Robert Reidt,
a peripatetic housepainter, paperhanger
lacking all peripheral doubts. He's prepared,
selling his house and his winter's worth of potatoes.
Cash in the afterlife still important.
At midnight Friday, he says, those who are the brides
of the Lamb will turn their faithful eyes to the east
and they shall see the sign mounted on a dark cloud,
surrounded by brilliant light that shall blind the eyes
of the wicked to deprive them of their sight.
And the 144,000 will be raised up and brought
to the woods outside San Diego with a short stop
on planet Jupiter, for the holy shall not travel on the Sabbath.
The wretched remaining will be reduced to ashes,
twisted into knots of disease, punched, battered, beat
with fist-sized hailstones, devoured by crawling pestilence.

In East Patchogue, Long Island, in the glare of the cameras,
moments before midnight, Robert Reidt missed the sign,
the beam of light, the savior-laden cloud,
as he stood hell-deep in reporters
and camera men. He knew the Lord was
on his way to earth and five days later, in a radio
broadcast from the Roosevelt Hotel, he wouldn't
give five cents for the Woolworth Building,
knowing the fireball about to strike New York City.
Over the months, kids back in school,
he continued to hang walls of forlorn paper.

3

April 21, 2011

My mom told me without doubt that I'm not going
to get into heaven on May 21st, 2011. It made me sad,
but it's what she believes. She'd quit her nursing job.
My dad sold the house. They were ready and ready
to drive their beliefs down the road. We're living out
of one of those whale-sized '70s station wagons.
From suburb to town to street fair to farmer's market,
we sound the trumpet of the end and hand out blurry
photocopied tracts. My parents happily say their final
goodbyes to friends and strangers till I'm bored.
We sell doomsday T-shirts to pay for gas,
looming black print that drips DOOM.
We can't make summer plans, there won't be one.
That's what we're told over and over,
until we no longer hear what they say.
Anyway, they'll be gone, two puddles of clothes
where they once stood, while me, my brother
and sister, will be here for the plagues, the quakes,
the wars, the famine. Not much different, really,
from what's happening right now.
If my mother tells me to get cleaned up,
I laugh, and tell her what's the difference
if the world's going to end. I'll be at a friend's
birthday party Saturday night, and either way,
I'm not sure I'll have parents to return to.

4

May 19, 2011:

There's so little time left. I'm glad God's
in charge. Believe me, Harold Camping isn't.
I couldn't possibly keep up with all the radio
interviews. We've bought 5,500 billboards,
including 400 in India, printed 100 million pamphlets
in 61 languages, and have 20 RVs driving 24-7
spreading the word. Family Radio Worldwide
broadcasts to the farthest corners—AM, FM, low-power,
and television—even though we're headquartered
between a custom auto-body shop that specializes
in metallic-flecked paint jobs and a tarot-reading psychic
who keeps offering us free introductory palm readings
here in Oakland, CA. We just keep waving our Bibles.
We're about to shut down the phone lines,
there's just too much joyful weeping,
we all have our crosses to bare and bear.
Every hill in San Francisco is a Calvary
with or without good brake pads.
I've calculated that Saturday is the 7000th anniversary
of that first rocking-in-the-waves star Noah
and he didn't need any guitar, codpiece,
glittering spandex, though he did have big hair
enough to upstage Kiss and Aerosmith together.
It's these millennia of sins that's sinking us
again but this time 200 million of us
are headed upstairs and naked to boot.

5

May 21, 2011:

6

May 22, 2011:

It was a really tough weekend.
Judgment day has come and passed, but it was
a spiritual judgment on the world.
There is no more salvation. Salvation is over.

God is God. God's going to do what he has to do.

It's right, it's good, we just don't understand how.

God delayed judgment so more people could be saved
and now we really know that will be October 21st, 2011,
when the world ends, ends, ends.

In 1844, when the world ended: . . . we wept and wept
all night until we could weep no more.

7

May 30, 2011:

This afternoon, Memorial Day, I relax
and listen, the turntable spins vinyl and that crazily eclectic,
sixties group, the Incredible String Band, kazoo
and sitar playing hoedown rhythms in the song
"Log Cabin in the Sky," as they sing, *We ain't got no home
in this world anymore*, give or take a day or two.

Boonville Bridge Demolition

March 2, 1998

1

The Water Street Park has half an Indian mound
left along the bluff above the river—bulldozers
and city elders haven't taken up the challenge.

Children race up and down its slope without
thought of what's underfoot, small voices
declaring this their summit, defending against

intruders, as once before long ago. They follow
their mothers' voices home across leafy backyards,
past paint-peeling porches, where drunks

easily recline, sleeping off another hostile encounter,
certain the stars are falling, but not far enough
to make a difference, though once or twice

they startle awake to the sucking gravity
of a chilly night. Other evenings expectant
lovers wait on the backside of this green knoll

to fondle their hopes and perhaps remember
what endures, holding tight to the close-cropped

2

grass. March morning winds wind up, strike

in volleys, in snow flurries, and a day dissolves

before it begins—not over those lovers
of the destitute or destitute lovers, veterans

of triumph and despair, but over crowds
gathering to watch while warming hands in coat
pockets and around coffee cups as children tug

at their parents, complaining of cold.
These apocalyptic sentinels standing on the mound
craning for a better view, as if the rumor

of a golden age was paddle-wheeling upriver
with god-like men brandishing the sword
of judgment and the horn of plenty,

and it happened that way nearly two centuries ago,
when the town gathered on burial mounds,
horses tied to trees, spoke-wheeled wagons parked

on the rutted road, convinced of the second coming,
and then the third, ad infinitum to heaven,
until the end of the waiting world did come

and they returned to their ashen hearths for salvation,
gathering kindling, striking flints. Today the crowd too
awaits destruction, dressed in overcoats and tennis shoes,

watching as men walk rusty girders high above
the wide muddy surge, ignoring the gusts or believing
in their immortal flight as they run wires back

to detonators and set gas charges designed to cut loose
steel convergences. It's past time for a final

3

crossing on old Route 5, once the only road
between the graft and corruption of distant cities,
and in the thirties local police waited at one end
of the bridge, barricaded in an upturned rusty steamboat

boiler, aiming tommy guns through small slits,
hoping for a chance at Pretty Boy Floyd escaping another
bank robbery, death the heart of headlines and fame,

or the smaller rites of passage as teenagers with their first
driver's licenses, faced the narrow bridge afraid,
its pavement not pavement but metal grates

with a view of the roiling river, and polished
by traffic the steel had a current of its own,
grabbing tires, setting cars on a course

to the murky bottom or the opposite lane,
the young drivers knew they held something

4

more than a license once having crossed.
The warning horn blares unnaturally across
the bottoms, as if the wet, thousand-mile-long
beast rolled over once more in agony

anticipating the fall, the channeling from mountain
to sea, and then the entanglement, the trap,
the black blast's staccato through triangulated

and arched spans. It could be a holiday celebration,
the pyrotechnics sparkling design hung in midair,
but for the ripping and tearing, the metallic groan,

so much giving way as the middle span collapses
after the many years of holding up both sides
of the river, then a seething uprising foam,

water churning above the abrupt sinking.
The current smoothes what is quickly memory.
The unbridgeable air clears of acrid smoke,

the crowds that waited hours for fog to lift,
hear the echoing concussion off the slate-clouded
underbelly, felt their own soft bodies' tremble,

their bones go soft, the day tenuous,
the aftermath of all their crossings uncrossed.